For Maja, to start cooking
on the right foot

Mavis Gallant

August 1984

EUROPEAN
CHOICE

EUROPEAN CHOICE

Good and Simple Recipes

Ruth Michaelis-Jena

CANONGATE

First published in 1977
by Canongate Publishing Limited
17 Jeffrey Street,
Edinburgh

© *Ruth Michaelis-Jena 1977*
Illustrations © *Thomas R. Breheny 1977*

ISBN 0 903937 50 6

Typeset by G. Sanderson (Phototypesetting),
44 Constitution Street, Leith, Edinburgh

Printed and bound in Great Britain by
Morrison & Gibb Ltd, London and Edinburgh

Contents

Introduction

To me nothing is more evocative than tastes and smells. Therefore it is perhaps natural that, as life goes on, I turn more and more to a bundle of faded papers, recipes collected by my mother more than fifty years ago. With the help of them I can conjure up the tastes and smells of my childhood, and I wallow in happy nostalgia.

Mine was a childhood not just far away in time, but far away in place and in manners. I was born within earshot of a busy market place where twice a week—summer and winter—peasants from the surrounding countryside came to offer their produce. The market began at seven o'clock in the morning, and from five o'clock onwards we could hear the clatter of horse-drawn carts and the heavy steps of people walking, carrying loaded baskets. Some even had baskets strapped to their backs. Carts and baskets were full of fruit and vegetables, all spring and summer gathered freshly that morning. Their scents wafted up to our open windows. Butter was offered fresh from the churn and eggs from hens which scratched field and farmyard for their feed. These hens, once too old to lay, were brought in wicker cages, as was other poultry for sale to be slaughtered by the customer only shortly before they went into the pot.

Freshness was the keyword then when it came to the buying of food, and although vitamins were little known, and 'diet' meant food for the sick, freshness was supposed to be 'good for you'. Even the country children who gathered mushrooms and herbs, brambles, rose-hips and blaeberries in season, shouted their wares as being 'freshly gathered'. Of course, we went ourselves on berry-gathering expeditions, and great feasts they were.

Tins were practically unknown in our household though my

1

mother bottled and pickled right through the summer to make sure of a variety of food in winter. Root vegetables were kept, dug into sand, in a deep, dark cellar where wooden bins held potatoes bought by the sackful in the autumn, and apples were stored on 'airing shelves'. Farm cheese was rather the rule than the exception, and, of course, good wholemeal bread, the darker the better. There were feather-light rolls for breakfast and crisp white bread. Milk came fresh from the cow, and buttermilk and cream cheese arrived fresh from the farm twice a week. Glasses of buttermilk quenched the thirst at any time, while cream cheese mixed with chives or caraway seeds, and spread on brown bread, made many a summer supper, followed often by a bowl of wild strawberries.

With all this abundance, nothing was ever wasted. My mother had developed the using of left-overs into a fine art.

In those distant days men and children were not welcome in the kitchen. Even the *gnädige Frau*—the gracious lady—of the household was only there on suffrance by cook or kitchen maid. My mother always insisted on doing the cooking herself, but I was never asked to join her. It seems, however, that not through observation but through subconscious absorbing, I even now find myself doing things the way she did. I use left-overs of meat, fish, vegetables, rice, pasta and cheese in all kinds of salads, soups or toasted sandwiches. I still like her mixtures of sweet and savoury: raisins, apples, pears and nuts mingling with onions, chutney, spiced herring or Parma ham in one and the same salad. Stale bread is never wasted. It makes puddings, provides toasted breadcrumbs or thickening for soups and sauces where I hardly ever use flour. I still prefer yolks of eggs— whites can always be used for the meringue-covering of a sweet—or cream to any other thickening agent, and would rather try and save on something else.

This, too, I believe, goes back to my mother always preferring the real thing to substitutes. Her lifespan included wars and spells of want through inflation, yet even then her cooking remained good though of necessity it had to be simple. My liking for fresh herbs and spices rather than artificial flavourings also goes back to my childhood. I am often asked which herbs I use in which dishes, and my embarrassed reply is that, more or less, I use them all and with everything. I use some not usually counted among culinary herbs, southernwood, the Scottish apple-ringie, for example, in salads. It is slightly sharper than taragon, and actually belongs to the same plant family. The leaves of scented verbena are good in apple sauce and fruit jellies. I am fortunate in having herbs grow just a few steps away from my kitchen, and I do dry them for winter. There is a list at the end of this book for those who wish to use herbs in a more orderly and conventional manner. I keep a vanilla pod in a jar of sugar. The sugar takes on the vanilla flavour, and a new pod is needed only from time to time. I cook all vegetables in very little water, adding a pinch of sugar to most of them in place of salt. I also like a little sugar in my salad dressings and herb sauces. Wherever possible, I peel neither apples nor potatoes. After cooking any kind of pasta, I put it on a sieve and let cold water run over it before finishing its preparation. This keeps the pasta from going mushy, keeps it *al dente,* as the Italians say. My pepper is the black kind and salt is natural sea salt. I always keep plain yoghourt ready for flavouring certain dishes and, when available, sour cream. I make many soups without using meat or bones, by browning a chopped onion in butter, then adding whatever vegetables are at hand. A teaspoonful of good yeast extract, stirred into the hot soup before serving, will supply that extra little flavour sometimes needed. A spoonful of sherry is an improvement not to soups only but to many other dishes.

With fish I like to be adventurous, and I often buy the not so popular varieties. All fish, I think, is better on the bone, even though fillets are convenient. When I do not fry or grill, I poach my fish in a court-bouillon, and this is my mother's recipe: Bring to the boil in a covered saucepan—but do not actually boil—equal parts of water and wine vinegar or white wine, cider will do, one scraped and cubed carrot, one sliced onion, one bay leaf, thyme, parsley and salt. Simmer for a little, then add a few peppercorns before putting in the fish. Mother also had a good basic recipe for mayonnaise: One egg yolk, one teaspoonful of lemon juice, pepper, salt and olive oil. While beating—in a deep bowl—the yolk, lemon juice, pepper and salt, olive oil is added drop by drop, beating until the sauce thickens. This can be made into a 'green sauce' by adding finely chopped herbs. Beating in one direction only, with a silver fork or wooden spoon, is essential. An electric blender is often used nowadays, but then the oil should be added not in drops but in a thin trickle, keeping the whisk always going. The electric blender may, in fact, be used wherever the old recipes recommend 'rubbing through a sieve'. It is also very efficient in making blended fruit drinks.

These then are my 'eating idiosyncrasies', and I also consider careful planning and shopping of great importance. Quality matters as well as price, and bulk buying may not always be the answer. A reliable butcher, fishmonger and greengrocer remain essential.

At a time when we are returning to greater simplicity, paying renewed interest to fresh, if possible home-grown vegetables, to cheaper cuts of meat and to unusual kinds of fish, these old recipes seem just right. They show that simple but good ingredients, handled with 'love', can make an excellent meal. They show that a meatless day need not be dull. The Continental housewife has the deserved reputation of being more frugal than her British counterpart, often able to make a plain meal look and taste attractive.

All my mother's recipes were collected on the Continent within her own family or while travelling. I have tried them all over many years, and have added a good few from my own experience of eating in different countries. They, too, are now in regular use in my kitchen. Travel and working abroad have brought the dishes of France, Germany, Holland, the Balkans, the Mediterranean and Scandinavian countries, even of Russia within many people's reach. The *cassoulet* of southern France, the *sauerkraut* of the German beer garden, the many *pastas* of Italy and a good thick *bortsch* can quite easily be prepared at home. The recipes of this book are meant for about four people but may be changed according to individual requirements.

Bon Appétit!

Ruth Michaelis-Jena
The Lang Hoose, East Saltoun
Summer 1977

Minestrone

1 lb. beef	3 tomatoes
1 thick slice gammon	1 onion
(if desired)	1-2 potatoes
1 cup haricot beans	1 cup rice or pasta
(previously soaked overnight	1 clove garlic
and par-cooked)	a little basil
2 cups shelled peas	pinch sugar
half a medium-size cabbage	olive or vegetable oil
3-4 carrots	pepper and salt

Chop onion and garlic and brown with meat in heated oil. Add water and bring slowly to the boil. Cut up all vegetables and put in with rice, except for the peas which need shorter cooking. If pasta is used instead of rice, this should be cooked with the mixture only for the last twenty minutes. Season and keep simmering until all ingredients are tender. Remove meat which may be made into a separate dish. Serve the thick soup very hot and sprinkle each individual portion with grated Parmesan cheese.

Bean Soup

1½ cups haricot beans	1 stick celery
1 onion	pepper and salt
1 tblsp. butter	

Soak beans overnight in cold water. Brown chopped onion and celery in butter, add beans and the water they have been soaked in. Simmer gently for two to three hours, adding water when necessary. Season well, rub through sieve, re-heat and serve very hot.

A tablespoon of sherry stirred in before serving, much improves this soup.

Potato and Celery Soup

2 heads celery	1 tblsp. butter
6 medium-size potatoes	pepper and salt

Chop celery finely and brown in butter. Add peeled potatoes and water to cover. Simmer gently until tender. Season, rub through sieve, re-heat and serve.

Stock may be used instead of water. If cooked without stock, the flavour is improved by adding a little yeast extract.

French Onion Soup

6 cups beef stock
3-4 large onions
1 tblsp. butter
1 clove

1 bay leaf
pinch brown sugar
pepper (black) and salt

Peel the onions, chop and cook gently in heated butter until transparent and light brown. Season, adding clove, bay leaf and pinch of sugar. Heat the stock, pour it over the mixture and keep simmering for some forty minutes.

This dish is enriched by frying a dry slice of bread for each portion—some ten minutes before serving—sprinkling the fried bread with grated cheese, and placing it into the bottom of each plate before pouring over the soup. The soup may also be poured into fireproof bowls, with the fried bread sprinkled with cheese floating on top. The bowls are then placed under the grill for a minute or two until the cheese is bubbling and turning brown.

Soup of fresh Green Peas with Egg Dumplings

6 cups beef stock
2 lb. peas
2 potatoes

2 tblsp. butter
pinch sugar
salt

For the dumplings

2 slices white bread	pinch nutmeg
1 egg	a little flour
butter	pepper and salt
a little milk	

Pod peas, peel potatoes and slice. Cook vegetables in stock until tender, adding a pinch of sugar and a little butter to bring out flavour. Season.

For the dumplings: Cream remainder of butter over steam and mix with egg, flour and bread, previously soaked in milk and squeezed out. Season, form into small dumplings and cook in slowly boiling soup for five minutes, keeping lid off.

Bortsch

3-4 large beetroot	1 large onion
1 tblsp. butter or	1 stick celery
vegetable oil	squeeze lemon juice
(left-overs of fat	pepper and salt
bacon or a beef	sour cream
marrow-bone may	
be used instead)	

Wash and par-boil beetroot, sufficient to be able to peel them. Shred finely together with the raw celery. Brown chopped onion in heated fat, add beetroot and celery mixture. Cover with water and simmer gently until beetroot is quite tender, adding more water if necessary. Season with lemon juice, pepper and salt. Rub through sieve, and serve very hot, adding a teaspoon of sour cream to each portion.

Tomato Soup with Rice

3-4 large tomatoes
1 small onion
1 sprig of thyme
1 tblsp. butter or
vegetable oil

pinch sugar
2 tblsp. rice
4-5 cups water
pepper and salt

Chop onion, quarter skinned tomatoes and crush. Cook the mixture gently in butter to which thyme has been added. When soft, rub through sieve and return to saucepan, add rice and water, a pinch of sugar, and season. Simmer slowly until rice is cooked but not mushy. Serve very hot.

The soup is improved by binding it with the yolk of an egg. Grated cheese may be served with each individual portion.

Julienne
Soup of Spring Vegetables

2 carrots
1 small white turnip
2 potatoes
1 leek
a few crisp cabbage leaves

1 cup shelled peas
1 tblsp. butter
pepper and salt
pinch sugar

Clean vegetables.
Cut carrots, turnip, potatoes, leek and cabbage leaves into thin strips about one centimetre long. Brown in melted butter,

11

add peas and cover well with water. Add a pinch of sugar and keep simmering gently until vegetables are tender, but not too soft. Season (using a little yeast extract, if desired).

Stock may be used instead of water, leaving out the yeast extract.

Clear Soup with Egg Garnish

6 cups good stock	pinch nutmeg
1 egg	salt
2 tblsp. milk	chives

Break egg and season with salt and nutmeg. Beat well with milk and pour into boiling stock. Cook for two minutes, sprinkle with finely chopped chives and serve at once.

Consommé with Marrow Dumplings

6 cups good beef stock	a little flour
2 thick slices white bread	pinch nutmeg
1 egg	pepper and salt
the marrow from a good-size beef marrow bone	parsley

Soak bread in water and squeeze out well. Cream the marrow over steam and mix with bread, egg and seasoning, using the flour to bind. Let the mixture cool, then form small dumplings. Cook these gently in hot stock for about six minutes, keeping lid off saucepan to prevent dumplings from breaking. Serve hot, garnished with chopped parsley.

Sweetbread Soup

4-5 cups stock	1 potato
1-2 calf's sweetbread	a little butter
1 onion	pepper and salt
2 carrots	

Soak the sweetbreads in cold water for two to three hours, changing the water once or twice. Then put them into a saucepan with cold water and bring to the boil. Dry in a colander, put on a flat dish and remove bits of skin and fat. Chop onion and fry in butter till golden brown. Slice other vegetables and add together with stock and cubed sweetbreads. Simmer gently for about half an hour, adding a little water if necessary. When sweetbreads are quite tender, serve very hot.

Asparagus tips cooked with this soup for the last five to ten minutes improves the flavour.

Cold Wine Soup

3-4 cups water	2 eggs
1-1½ cups white	1 small tblsp. cornflour
wine or cider	a little vanilla
2 tblsp. sugar	a little ground cinnamon

Heat water with sugar. Make cornflour, yolks of eggs and a touch of vanilla into a smooth paste with cold liquid. Stir gently into the heated water, add wine and bring to the boil. Beat whites of eggs stiff and drop spoonfuls on to the hot mixture. Remove from fire when the whites have set.

Serve chilled with a little cinnamon sprinkled over the egg whites.

Dandelion Salad

2 handfuls young
   dandelion leaves
1 small onion

1 tblsp. olive oil
squeeze lemon juice

   Wash and trim leaves. Dry, then make a dressing of oil, lemon juice and finely chopped onion. Shred leaves and mix with the dressing.

   No pepper or salt is needed as the dandelion leaves have a very distinct flavour of their own.

Mixed Salad

1 carrot
1 stick celery
1 small white turnip
1 medium-size onion
1 red pepper
1 piece cucumber

1 apple
juice of half a lemon
2 tblsp. olive oil
pinch sugar
salt

Wash and chop up all raw vegetables, using the apple cored but not peeled. Make up dressing and pour over vegetables. Serve at once.

Andalusian Salad

1 lettuce
2 oranges
2 tblsp. mayonnaise

2 slices fresh (or tinned) pineapple
a little sugar

Wash and dry lettuce. Put leaves into salad bowl. Peel and slice oranges, add pineapple. Spread fruit mixture on lettuce, and pour over mayonnaise to which a little sugar has been added.

The salad may be decorated with hard-boiled eggs or grated cheese.

Tomato Salad

3-4 medium-size tomatoes
1 small onion
1 tblsp. vinegar
2 tblsp. olive oil

pinch sugar
pepper and salt
parsley
basil

Make dressing of vinegar, oil and seasoning. Slice onions very finely into rings. Mix the carefully separated rings with thinly sliced tomatoes and put into dressing. Sprinkle with basil and parsley. Let stand for twenty-four hours, and serve chilled.

Savoury Apple Salad

4 medium-size apples
1 onion
some shelled nuts
pinch sugar

juice of half a lemon
2 tblsp. olive oil
pepper and salt

Wash apples but do not peel. Core and slice thinly. Chop onion, and make a dressing of lemon juice, oil, sugar, pepper and salt.

Mix with apples and onions and garnish with nuts.

Grated cheese may be added, if desired.

Cabbage Salad with Peanut Dressing

1 small firm white cabbage
2 apples
2 tblsp. chopped peanuts

1 cup yoghourt
1 tsp. brown sugar
a little paprika

Wash, trim and shred cabbage. Wash and grate apple, mix with cabbage. Make dressing of peanuts, yoghourt and rest of ingredients. Pour over cabbage mixture and allow to stand for a little before serving.

If desired, the leaves of the cabbage may be softened by standing them over steam for a few minutes, before being cut up.

Salad of Carrots

6 medium-size
    young carrots
3 medium-size apples
2 tblsp. olive oil

juice of a lemon
a little sugar
some grated cheese
parsley

Clean carrots and grate. Wash and core apples and grate with their peel. Mix with carrots.

Make dressing of lemon juice, oil and sugar. Pour over the salad and sprinkle with grated cheese and chopped parsley.

Cucumber Salad

1 medium-size cucumber	1 small onion
1 tblsp. vinegar	a little parsley
2 tblsp. olive oil	pepper and salt

Peel cucumber and slice thinly. Place in bowl, sprinkle with salt and cover with cold water. Drain after about half an hour, and carefully squeeze cucumber in a clean towel. Make dressing of vinegar, oil, grated onion, chopped parsley, pepper and salt. Pour over the cucumber, mix and serve at once.

A leaf or two of borage, finely chopped, improves the flavour of cucumber salad.

Kohlrabi and Tomato Salad

4 tender kohlrabi	pinch sugar
4-6 tomatoes	a little dill
juice of half a lemon	(green, finely chopped,
1 tsp. mild mustard	or dry powdered)
1 cup yoghourt	pepper and salt
2 tblsp. olive oil	

Peel kohlrabi, slice. Cut a thin slice off the tops of tomatoes, and scoop out pulp carefully. Make a dressing of yoghourt, olive oil, lemon juice, sugar, mustard, pepper, salt and tomato pulp. Whip to creamy consistency and pour over kohlrabi. Garnish with tomato slices, taken from the tops and dill. Serve chilled.

Salad of Lettuce and Nasturtium Leaves

1 lettuce
2 hard-boiled eggs
a handful nasturtium leaves
2 tblsp. olive oil

juice of half a lemon
pinch sugar
salt
finely chopped chives

Wash and dry lettuce. Break leaves by hand and add nasturtium leaves. Make up dressing and pour over salad. Garnish with quartered eggs and sprinkle with chives.

Potato Salad

6 medium-size potatoes
2 tblsp. olive oil
1 tblsp. wine vinegar

½ onion
½ tsp. sugar
pepper and salt

Boil potatoes in their jackets—do not let them go too soft—drain, peel and slice. Make up dressing of rest of ingredients and pour over potatoes while still hot.

The salad is best if allowed to stand overnight in a cool place.

Garnish with chopped parsley, chives, cut tomatoes or hard-boiled eggs.

Spinach Salad

2 handfuls fresh
  tender spinach
1 small clove garlic

2 tblsp. olive oil
squeeze lemon juice
very little sugar
salt

Wash and trim spinach. Dry well. Make a dressing of oil, lemon juice, finely chopped garlic, sugar and salt. Shred the spinach, mix with dressing and serve at once.

Apples and Potatoes 'Heaven and Earth'

3 medium-size apples
3 medium-size potatoes
pinch salt

3 whole cloves
1 tblsp. sugar

Peel and slice apples and cook gently with sugar and cloves.

Peel and cook potatoes in water to which a little salt has been added.

Mash potatoes when soft and mix on a low fire with apple sauce.

Serve with fried or grilled meats; particularly good with liver and bacon.

Globe Artichokes with Egg and Onion Dip

1 good-size artichoke per person

Ingredients for dip

2 hard-boiled eggs
1 onion
4 tblsp. olive oil
juice of a lemon

a little mild mustard
pinch sugar
parsley
pepper and salt

Wash and trim artichokes and plunge them head down into fast-boiling water to which a little lemon juice and salt have been added. Simmer for some twenty minutes. Probe with fork, and when the artichoke bottoms are tender, drain and let cool.

Make dressing by carefully blending oil, lemon juice, mustard, pinch of sugar, pepper and salt. Then add onion and hard boiled eggs, chopped finely.

Serve artichokes well cooled with dip in a separate bowl.

Jerusalem Artichokes au Gratin

1 lb. Jerusalem artichokes
1 small onion
1 tblsp. butter
½ cup cream

1 cup grated cheese
pinch nutmeg
pepper and salt

Wash artichokes in plenty of water, scrub well but do not peel. Put them into saucepan with just enough water to cover. Steam and when parboiled, rub off skins of artichokes. Place in a buttered oven dish, pour over cream, season with grated nutmeg, onion, pepper and salt. Cover dish and cook in a hot oven for about half an hour. Then take off lid, sprinkle with cheese and brown for another five to ten minutes.

A mixture of powdered herbs may be added to the cheese, if desired.

Broad Beans

1 lb. broad beans	pinch brown sugar
3-4 rashers bacon	pepper and salt
1 tblsp. butter	parsley
2 tblsp. flour	

Put the shelled beans into water to which a pinch of brown sugar has been added. Bring to the boil and cook for some eight minutes. Dice bacon and crisp up in frying pan. Make a white sauce with flour, butter and a little vegetable water. Drain beans and put into sauce with the crisped-up bacon. Season and simmer until beans are tender. Sprinkle with chopped parsley before serving.

French Beans 'Sweet-sour'

1 lb. French beans
1 apple
juice of a lemon

1 tsp. butter
2 tsp. brown sugar
parsley

Wash and string beans, slice and put into saucepan. Cover with water and boil until tender. Drain, add lemon juice, sugar, butter and peeled and sliced apple. Simmer gently for five to ten minutes. Add chopped parsley and toss over fire.

Delicious with sauté potatoes, and a good accompaniment to roast pork.

Beetroot in Cream Sauce

6 medium-size beetroot
juice of a lemon
1 tblsp. flour
1 tblsp. butter
½ cup creamy milk

1 small onion
1 bay leaf
pinch brown sugar
pepper and salt

Wash and parboil beetroot. Peel and slice. Make a sauce of flour, milk, butter, lemon juice, finely chopped onion, seasoning with sugar, pepper, salt and bay leaf. Put beetroot slices into sauce and finish cooking for some twenty minutes in moderate oven.

Remove bay leaf before serving.

Brussels Sprouts cooked in Butter

2 lb. Brussels sprouts   pinch grated nutmeg
1 tblsp. butter   pepper and salt

Blanch prepared Brussels sprouts for about five minutes. Drain, put into buttered casserole with a little of the vegetable water. Season with pepper, salt and nutmeg. Dot with small pieces of butter. Cover and cook in a moderate oven till tender but not too soft.

Cabbage Casserole

1 medium-size cabbage   1 tblsp. butter
1 onion   mixed herbs
1 lb. steak mince   pepper and salt

Wash cabbage, remove any wilted outer leaves and blanch for about five minutes. Dry and put into casserole alternate layers of cabbage and mince—mixed with chopped onion, herbs, pepper and salt—finishing with a layer of cabbage.

Cook in covered casserole for about one hour in a moderate oven. For the last ten minutes remove lid of casserole, dot top layer with little lumps of butter, and let brown. Serve with boiled potatoes.

The mince may be replaced by savoury rice with chopped-up hard-boiled eggs or cheese and red peppers, in fact any vegetarian mixture.

Red Cabbage

1 medium-size red cabbage
2 cooking apples
1 tblsp. butter
1 glass red wine

1 tsp. brown sugar
2-3 whole cloves
pinch salt

Wash and finely shred cabbage. Put into saucepan in which butter has been slightly browned. Shake cabbage in butter for two to three minutes. Add apple (washed, cored and sliced), seasoning and enough water to cover. Cook very slowly for an hour to an hour and a half.

Savoy or White Cabbage in Savoury Sauce

1 cabbage
1½ tblsp. butter
1 tblsp. flour

caraway seeds
pepper and salt

Wash and cut cabbage, removing tough leaves and stalks.
Soak for a few minutes in salted water. Put into saucepan with very little water and a dot of butter. Cook over gentle heat until tender, only adding a little water if necessary. Make sauce of flour, butter and a little vegetable water. Season and put cabbage back into this.
Finish cooking over a low flame and serve very hot.

Chicory

4-6 heads chicory
2 tblsp. butter

squeeze lemon juice
pepper and salt

Wash chicory and remove coarse outer leaves. Cook, uncovered, in boiling water, to which a little lemon juice has been added until tender. Drain, season and turn in melted butter.

Serve very hot.

Fried Egg Plant (Aubergine)

3-4 egg plants
1 tblsp. flour
1 tblsp. olive oil

1 cup grated Parmesan
  cheese
salt

Peel the egg plants and slice—about two centimetres thick—turn the slices in flour to which a little salt has been added. Fry in olive oil until golden brown. Sprinkle with cheese and serve very hot.

Tomato purée may be served with the egg plants.

Fennel au Gratin

2 good-size fennel roots
1 cup grated cheese
1 tblsp. cream

a little butter
pepper and salt

Peel and slice the fennel roots and tender parts of stalks. Cook in boiling water, just enough to cover, until tender. Drain and put into buttered casserole. Cover with cream and grated cheese. Season, and brown under grill.

Hot-Pot of Black Lentils

2-3 cups black lentils
1 onion (stuck with cloves)
1 stick celery
2 potatoes

1 garlic ring (smoked
  Continental sausage)
parsley

Soak lentils overnight. Prepare onion, celery and potatoes, put them into saucepan with lentils, adding a little more water if necessary. All ingredients should be well covered. Bring to the boil, then, lowering flame, cook slowly for two to three hours. Put in sausage for the last twenty minutes only. Simmer gently and see that all the water has been absorbed. Lift out sausage ring, dice and return to dish.

Serve very hot, sprinkled with parsley.

Macaroni with Mushrooms

½ lb. macaroni
½ lb. mushrooms
1 egg
½ cup milk or cream

1 tblsp. butter
1 tblsp. breadcrumbs
½ cup grated cheese
pepper and salt

Clean mushrooms and cook in melted butter. Cook macaroni in slightly salted water until tender—but not too soft—approximately fifteen to twenty minutes. Drain well. Mix macaroni and the prepared mushrooms. Place in a buttered casserole. Switch up egg, milk, pepper and salt, and pour over mixture. Sprinkle with breadcrumbs and grated cheese. Bake for half an hour in a moderate oven.

Vegetable Marrow

1 medium-size marrow or a few small courgettes
2 tblsp. olive oil

For the stuffing:

2 hard-boiled eggs,
   chopped finely
1 small tin tomato purée
½ cup cooked rice

1 clove garlic
marjoram
pinch sugar
pepper and salt

Wash marrow—do not peel—cut lengthwise and remove seeds. Parboil gently. Lift and fill with well-mixed stuffing. Heat olive oil in casserole, add stuffed marrow, and finish cooking in moderate oven for some twenty minutes.

Onions au Gratin

4-6 good-size
Spanish onions
1 cup milk
1 tblsp. butter

1 cup grated cheese
pinch oregon
pepper and salt

Boil onions till almost tender. Lift and drain. Put into buttered casserole. Season and cover with milk and grated cheese. Brown in a quick oven or under the grill.

Serve very hot.

Peas and Carrots

2 lb. peas
1 lb. carrots
2 tsp. butter

pinch sugar
salt

Clean and cook sliced or cubed carrots. Shell peas and add when carrots are almost tender, together with a pinch of sugar. Continue cooking until peas are done. Shake with butter over a low fire, and serve at once.

Stuffed Peppers

6 peppers
1 onion
1 small tin tomato purée or
    two large tomatoes, skinned
    and sieved

3 cups cooked mince
    (this may be replaced by
    savoury rice)
1 tblsp. olive oil
a little butter
pinch sugar
a little rosemary

    Clean and prepare peppers, taking care that no seeds are left inside. Cut them into halves. Parboil for a few minutes, then place in a buttered casserole. Stuff with mince and cover with a sauce whipped up of tomato purée, oil, olive oil and seasoning. Bake in a hot oven for some ten to fifteen minutes.

Rösti-Swiss fried Potatoes

4-5 medium-size potatoes
2 tblsp. butter or vegetable oil
pepper and salt

    Boil potatoes in their jackets. Peel and slice thinly. Heat fat and add potatoes, pepper and salt. Fry on hot flame, turning potatoes all the time until golden brown. Lower heat, press down potatoes, and leave for another few minutes when crust will form underneath.

    Turn out on hot dish with the crust uppermost.

    Sprinkle with parsley, chives or finely chopped onion before serving.

Potato Dumplings

6 medium-size potatoes
2 tblsp. flour
1 egg
1 small onion

4 slices white bread
1 tblsp. butter
pinch grated nutmeg
salt

Peel and boil potatoes. Dry and let cool. Then rub them through sieve. Dice white bread and fry in butter, adding a little chopped onion. Mix croutons when nice and brown with potatoes and rest of ingredients.

Form dumplings and plunge into boiling salted water. Cook slowly—with lid off saucepan—for some ten minutes. Fry more cubes of bread to serve poured over dumplings with the melted butter.

With a side salad dumplings make a good vegetarian meal. They may also accompany meat dishes.

Potato Pancakes

6-8 medium-size potatoes
2 eggs
½ cup warm milk
1 tblsp. flour

a little finely chopped onion
vegetable oil
pepper and salt

Peel and grate the raw potatoes. Squeeze out superfluous liquid. Mix milk with potatoes adding flour, eggs, onion, pepper and salt. Blend well with wooden spoon, and drop mixture from spoon into smoking oil. Fry for about four to five minutes on each side.

Serve at once.

The pancakes may accompany meat and vegetables but will make a meal by themselves when served with cheese, a savoury sauce, tuna fish or good helpings of apple sauce.

Parsley Potatoes

6-8 potatoes
1 onion
1 tblsp. flour
1 tblsp. vegetable oil

1 cup milk
½ cup finely chopped
    parsley
pepper and salt

Chop onion and fry in heated oil until golden brown. Reduce heat and make a sauce by adding flour, milk, pepper and salt. Add potatoes—previously peeled and sliced—simmer gently with lid on saucepan until potatoes are done. Add more liquid if necessary and stir well. Put in parsley and cook with the mixture for the last five minutes. Serve very hot.

Sauté Potatoes

6-8 medium-size potatoes
2 small onions
2 tblsp. butter or vegetable oil

pepper and salt
parsley

Boil potatoes—taking care not to overboil—chop onions and fry slightly. Peel potatoes when tender but not too soft, and add fairly thick slices to onions in frying pan. Cook until golden brown, turning potatoes frequently.

Sprinkle with parsley before serving. A peeled tomato included in the fry adds to the flavour.

Stuffed Potatoes

6 medium-size potatoes
4 rashers bacon (cubed and crisped up)
pinch grated nutmeg
pepper and salt
some mixed herbs (freshly chopped or dried)

Scrub potatoes—do not peel—and parboil gently. Remove from fire and scoop out centres. Mash the scooped-out parts and mix with bacon. Season and refill potatoes with mixture. Finish cooking in moderate oven for about fifteen minutes.

Bacon may be replaced by grated cheese.

Sauerkraut-Choucroûte

1 lb. sauerkraut
1 small onion
1 tblsp. vegetable oil

pinch brown sugar
a few dried juniper
    berries—if desired

Brown onion in heated oil. Add sauerkraut, previously loosened with fork. Cover with enough water to prevent burning (a tablespoon of white wine or cider improves the flavour). Cook very slowly for a couple of hours.

A garlic ring—smoked Continental sausage—cooked on top of the sauerkraut for the last fifteen minutes, and separately cooked mashed potatoes make this a complete and easily prepared meal.

Sauerkraut is readily available in tins or jars but can also be made at home:

2 firm white cabbages, water and salt are needed.

Remove tough outer leaves of cabbages, using hearts only. Wash and dry well.

Shred cabbages and put thin layers into a stone jar. Sprinkle each layer thickly with coarse salt. Knead and pack closely. Cover jar with linen cloth and place weight on top, e.g. big stone.

The sauerkraut will be fully pickled in three weeks. During this maturing period skim top of brine regularly and keep adding salt.

Purée of French Sorrel

2 lb. French sorrel	a little milk
1 tsp. butter	1 tblsp. sugar
1 tsp. flour	pepper and salt

Trim and wash sorrel, discarding corse leaves and stalks. Put into saucepan wet and cook on slow fire for some twenty-five minutes. Make sauce of butter, flour and milk. Season and put in sorrel, previously rubbed through a sieve. Serve very hot as an accompaniment to poached eggs or fried fish.

A spoonful of cream improves this dish.

Creamed Spinach

2 lb. spinach
1 small onion
1 tblsp. butter

1 tblsp. flour
pinch grated nutmeg
pepper and salt

Wash spinach in two or three lots of cold water. Put wet spinach into saucepan and cook covered for some five to seven minutes. No additional water is needed. Dry and cut or make into purée. Brown chopped onion in butter, add spinach, season and re-heat. Add a spoonful of cream before serving.

Creamed purée of spinach makes an excellent 'bed' for a poached egg.

MEAT AND POULTRY

Boiled Beef

2-3 lb. silverside	1 stick celery
2 carrots	1 tsp. butter
1 onion	mixed herbs
1 tomato	pepper and salt

    Brown finely chopped onion in butter, add meat and brown on both sides. Add water to cover and cut-up vegetables. Season and bring quickly to the boil.

    Lower flame, add herbs and keep simmering gently until meat is tender. Remove meat and pour over a little of the liquid. Serve with boiled potatoes, pickled gherkins or horseradish.

    Boiled beef may also be served in a white sauce, made of the juice of the meat with a little water, flour and chopped parsley.

Boeuf Bourguignon

1½ lb. good stewing steak
1 carrot
1 large onion
1 glass red wine

2 tblsp. butter
2 tblsp. flour
mixed herbs
pepper and salt

Cube steak and turn each cube in flour. Fry meat in heated butter, lower flame and add chopped onion, sliced carrot and herbs. Season, add wine and a little water. Cover closely and cook gently for 2-3 hours.

Esterhazy Steak

1-1½ lb. steak
  (preferably loin)
2 onions
1 parsnip

2 cups sour cream
1 tblsp. butter or
  vegetable oil
salt and paprika

Cube meat and fry in heated fat on both sides. In a separate dish fry sliced vegetables until golden brown. Put into saucepan with meat, season and pour over sour cream. Simmer gently in covered saucepan until all ingredients are tender.

Boeuf Strogonoff

1½ lb. filleted steak
1 onion
½ lb. small mushrooms

2 tblsp. butter
1 cup sour cream
pepper and salt

Cut the steak into strips, salt and pepper, and beat them very flat. Slice onions and mushrooms and cook in butter. Melt the remaining butter, and quickly fry the strips of steak in a separate pan. Mix steak with vegetables and slowly and carefully put in the sour cream. Heat gently—without boiling—and serve very hot, accompanied by a potato purée.

Goulash

1½-2 lb. stewing steak
3 tomatoes (or 1 small
    tin tomato purée)
2 onions
1 carrot

2 tblsp. butter
1 tblsp. flour
½ cup sour cream
a little paprika
salt

Cube meat and turn in flour to which a little salt has been added. Heat butter in saucepan and fry meat and chopped onions until golden brown. Then add sliced carrot, tomatoes and enough water to keep from burning. Simmer gently till tender. Season with paprika and put in sour cream just before serving.

A teaspoon of caraway seeds may be added, also half a glass of red wine, if desired.

Pickled Roast

1-2 lb. silverside
2-3 onions
1 carrot
2 bay leaves
mixed herbs

2-3 whole cloves
peppercorns
½ cup wine vinegar
salt

Bring to the boil about 1-1½ litres water, adding a little chopped onion, sliced carrot, bay leaves, herbs, peppercorns, salt and vinegar. Simmer for a few minutes. Put meat into deep bowl and strain liquid over it.

Cover bowl and leave in a cool place for three days. Fry onions in a casserole, when brown add meat and cover with marinade. Simmer gently for one or two hours. Serve very hot.

Grandmother's Cassoulet

1 lb. knuckle end
  leg of mutton
½ lb. loin of pork
1 piece French
  garlic sausage
a few rashers streaky bacon
1 lb. haricot beans
2-3 potatoes
1 stick celery

1 large onion
2 cloves garlic
1 small tin tomato purée
1 glass red wine
mixed herbs
2 tblsp. vegetable oil
pinch brown sugar
pepper and salt

Soak haricot beans overnight. Next morning simmer them in the water they have been soaked in for about an hour, adding a pinch of brown sugar. While the beans are cooking, par-roast the mutton in a moderate oven for about half an hour. Cut pork into strips. Cube bacon, crisp-up in frying pan, adding oil, sliced onion and pork stuck with garlic. Remove from fire when nice and brown. Fill deep casserole with alternate layers of beans, mixed with sliced raw potatoes and chopped celery, and cut-up mutton and pork, finishing with slices of garlic sausage. Mix tomato purée with red wine, the water the beans were cooked in and herbs. Pour over the mixture, previously seasoned with pepper and salt. Cook in a slow oven—covering the casserole—for some three hours. Lift lid for the last ten minutes to let top brown, if necessary adding a little more oil.

Casserole of Pork Chops

4 pork chops (not too fat)
2-3 skinned tomatoes
a handful cleaned mushrooms
1 tblsp. butter

1 clove garlic
1 glass white wine
a little flour
pepper and salt

Fry chops lightly in melted butter with the crushed clove of garlic. Then place them into deep casserole, with tomatoes, mushrooms and seasoning. Moisten with wine and extra water if necessary. Simmer until tender, and thicken with a little flour five minutes before serving.

Ragout of Lamb

1-1½ lb. stewing lamb   2 tblsp. butter or vegetable oil
4 potatoes   2 tblsp. flour
2 carrots   marjoram and rosemary
2 onions   pepper and salt

Cut meat into small pieces, turn in flour and fry in melted butter. When the meat is browned on both sides, cover with water and add sliced carrots, onions and mixed herbs. Season and cook gently for about an hour. Then add peeled and sliced potatoes and continue cooking until all ingredients are tender. Serve at once.

Carrots may be left out, if a few cooked asparagus tips are added just before serving.

Fricassee of Veal

1 lb. filleted veal
1 small onion
pinch ground ginger
squeeze of lemon juice or a little white wine
a little flour or one egg yolk
pepper and salt

Cut veal, previously rubbed with ginger, into small cubes, and fry in butter with sliced onion. Add very little water, a squeeze of lemon juice or one tablespoon of white wine. Season and simmer gently until veal is tender. Thicken juice with flour or an egg yolk, just before serving.

Mushrooms may be added, if desired.

Wiener Schnitzel

1 lb. filleted veal
1 egg
1 cup breadcrumbs

2 tblsp. butter
a little flour
pepper and salt

Cut the filleted veal into squares, beat them flat. Season. Then dip first in flour, after that in beaten egg and last in breadcrumbs. When evenly covered, fry gently in heated butter, on both sides, turning carefully once or twice.

Serve hot, garnished, if you like, with a slice of lemon, surmounted by a slice of hard-boiled egg on which is placed a rolled-up anchovy or a few capers.

Chicken with Rice

1 medium-size chicken
2 cups rice
1 onion, stuck with
    one or two cloves
1 egg yolk
mixed herbs
clove garlic

1 tblsp. butter
parsley
squeeze lemon
    juice and a little
    grated peel
pepper and salt

Clean chicken, put a little butter, grated lemon peel and a clove of garlic inside the chicken. Melt remaining butter in saucepan, turn chicken in this, frying lightly. Add giblets, onion, herbs and a squeeze of lemon juice. Season and cover with water. Bring to the boil and simmer gently until chicken is almost tender—approximately requiring another twenty minutes' cooking. Remove giblets, put in rice and continue cooking fast until rice is done. When ready, take out chicken, cut into pieces and keep hot while straining rice. Retain liquid and thicken with the yolk of an egg. Serve pieces of chicken on a bed of rice, covered with the sauce. Sprinkle with chopped parsley.

Ragout of Poultry

Pieces of chicken left-overs   a little flour
½ chicken liver or giblets   paprika
1 onion   salt
1 tblsp. butter

Brown sliced onion in butter, add giblets, fry lightly and sprinkle with a little flour. Season, cover with stock, previously made from the chicken bones. Simmer gently for an hour. Add left-overs of poultry for the last twenty minutes. Serve with pasta.

Mushrooms, tomatoes and a spoonful of white wine may be added to the ragout, if desired.

Breaded Sweetbreads

1 lb. sweetbreads
  (calf or lamb)
1 egg
2 tblsp. butter

½ cup breadcrumbs
a little flour
chopped chives
pepper and salt

Blanch sweetbreads in slightly salted water for some thirty minutes. Drain, cover with fresh water and simmer for about quarter of an hour. Removemembranes and slice. Dip slices in beaten egg, then in seasoned breadcrumbs to which a little flour has been added. Cook gently in heated butter till brown on both sides.

Serve sprinkled with chopped chives.

Kidneys in Madeira Sauce

3-4 kidneys (preferably
  sheep's or lamb's)
1 tblsp. butter
1½ tblsp. flour
1 cup washed and sliced mushrooms

1 clove garlic
½ cup Madeira wine
pepper and salt
chopped parsley

Skin kidneys, cut into halves and remove fat. Cut again into small pieces. Heat butter and fry pieces, taking care that they are browned on both sides. Add mushrooms and crushed garlic, sprinkle with flour, season and moisten with wine. Stir until the flour is blended and simmer gently on a low flame. Do not let boil. Serve hot, sprinkled with parsley.

Liver and Apples

1 lb. liver
2 cooking apples
1 onion
1½ tblsp. butter

1 tblsp. flour
a little brown sugar
pepper and salt

Wash and dry slices of liver and turn in flour to which a little pepper and salt have been added. Fry in butter till brown on both sides. Then add apples—cored and sliced, but not peeled—and chopped onion, with a little water to prevent burning. Simmer gently till tender in covered frying pan. Serve very hot with the apples arranged round the liver. Sprinkle apple slices with a touch of brown sugar.

Liver Dumplings

½ lb. liver
4 thick slices white bread
1 small onion
1 egg

2 tblsp. butter
1 tblsp. breadcrumbs
a little marjoram
pepper and salt

Soak bread in water and squeeze out when soft. Mince raw liver and mix with bread, adding butter (creamed over steam) and grated onion. Season, and let mixture cool before adding breadcrumbs flavoured with marjoram.

Form small balls and let stand for half an hour. Bring salted water to the boil and cook dumplings in it for some ten minutes. Remove and serve very hot accompanied by hot vegetables or a mixed salad.

Rissoles à la Königsberg

1 lb. mince (preferably beef and pork mixed)
2 slices white bread (soaked in water and squeezed out)
1 egg
2 tblsp. flour
1 tblsp. butter
juice of half a lemon or ½ glass white wine
pepper and salt

Mix well all ingredients—including some of the flour—and shape into small balls. Turn these in the remaining flour. Bring to the boil three to four cups of slightly salted water to which butter has been added. Cook rissoles in the liquid—keeping lid off saucepan—for twenty to twenty-five minutes. Flavour liquid with lemon juice or white wine, reduce, adding a little extra flour, if necessary. Serve rissoles with the sauce poured over them.

Capers may be added, if desired.

Meat Balls

½ lb. raw mince
½ lb. left-over roast, minced
2 thick slices white bread
2 eggs

1 tblsp. flour
1 tblsp. butter
pepper and salt
breadcrumbs

Soak bread in water and squeeze out when soft. Mix all ingredients well, season and form into rissoles. Turn in breadcrumbs and fry in heated butter, turning frequently. Onion rings or sliced tomatoes may be added to the fry.

Meat Loaf

½ lb. minced beef
½ lb. minced pork
2 eggs
2 thick slices white bread
1 onion

mixed herbs
a little grated lemon peel
1 tblsp. flour
pepper and salt

Soak bread in water and squeeze out when soft. Mix with mince, season and bind with flour and switched eggs. Shape the mixture into a loaf, put into greased roasting-tin and cook in a moderate oven for about an hour.

Baste frequently.

Extra flavour may be added to the loaf by using one teaspoon of caraway seeds in the mixture or two or three chopped-up anchovies.

Also, hard-boiled eggs may be put into the centre of the loaf.

Delicious served cold, sliced with salad.

Smoked Garlic Sausage with Curly Kale and Potatoes

1 handful curly kale
4-5 potatoes
1 garlic ring
  (smoked Continental sausage)

bay leaf
peppercorns
salt

Remove hard stalks from kale, wash and blanch for two or three minutes. Strain and chop finely. Put peeled and thickly sliced potatoes into deep saucepan, add peppercorns, bay leaf and salt, and mix in kale. Cover with just enough water to prevent burning. Bring to the 'boil, then reduce heat and continue cooking until potatoes are almost done, stirring occasionally. For the last ten minutes put sausage on top of vegetable mixture. Serve very hot, with a few slices of sausage to each portion.

The sausage may be sliced before putting into the saucepan, but then needs less cooking time. Small Frankfurters can be used instead of the garlic ring.

Bacon and Potato Savoury

5-6 good-size potatoes
¾ lb. shoulder bacon
2 tblsp. butter
1 tblsp. flour

1½-2 cups milk
pinch grated nutmeg
a little marjoram
pepper and salt

Make white sauce of flour, butter and milk. Season. Let cool slightly. Cube and crisp-up bacon, then add to sauce with a pinch of nutmeg, a little marjoram and peeled and thickly sliced potatoes.

Turn into a greased oven dish and cook in a moderate oven for about an hour. If too dry, dot with little lumps of butter ten minutes before ready.

Serve hot, sprinkled with chopped parsley.

Spaghetti Bolognese

½ lb. spaghetti	salt

Ingredients for sauce:

2 cups steak mince	a few button mushrooms
3-4 peeled tomatoes	2 tblsp. olive oil
or 1 small tin	½ glass red wine
tomato purée	basil
1 onion	pinch sugar
1 clove garlic	pepper and salt
1 stick celery	

Cook spaghetti in salted boiling water—not too soft—dry on colander. Then put into dish in which a little olive oil has been heated, and keep warm.

Prepare sauce beforehand:

Heat olive oil and in it fry quickly mince, chopped celery, mushrooms, onion and garlic. When mince is slightly brown, add tomatoes, pepper, salt and basil. Moisten with wine, finally adding a pinch of sugar. Continue simmering for some ten minutes, watching carefully that sauce keeps a creamy consistency. Pour the sauce over spaghetti and serve very hot.

Have a bowl of grated cheese—preferably Parmesan—ready for individual helpings.

Roast Goose, stuffed with Apples and Chestnuts

1 plump goose (some 10 to 12 lb.)
clove garlic
squeeze lemon juice
a little vegetable oil

For the stuffing:
the giblets, cooked and minced
1 lb. sausage meat
½ lb. boiled chestnuts
3-4 cooking apples, peeled, cored and sliced
a little thyme and sage
pinch brown sugar
pepper and salt

Clean and prepare goose, rubbing it with a little lemon juice.

Mix cooked giblets, sausage meat, boiled chestnuts and sliced raw apples with a pinch of brown sugar and seasoning. Stuff the goose with the mixture. Pour a little cooking oil over the bird and put into pre-heated oven. Cook for two to two and a half hours, basting frequently, and removing surplus fat from roasting dish. Prick the skin of the goose from time to time to release more fat. Serve when nice and crisp with its own juice.

Save goose fat which is an excellent seasoning for meat and vegetable casseroles.

Venison Casserole

1½ lb. filleted venison
2 tblsp. butter or
  or vegetable oil
2 tblsp. flour
1 clove garlic

1 cup mushrooms
  (cleaned and sliced)
1 glass red wine
mixed herbs
pepper and salt

Cube the venison, turn in flour and fry till brown on both sides, adding the crushed clove of garlic. Put into deep warmed casserole, with mushrooms, seasoning and herbs. Moisten with wine. Add a little water, if necessary. Cook slowly in a moderate oven for an hour or two, depending on the quality of the venison. When tender, serve at once with boiled potatoes.

FISH

Herring Salad

3-4 salt herrings
2 hard-boiled eggs
1 small onion
1 pickled gherkin
2 cooked beetroot

2 medium-size
  boiled potatoes
2 raw apples
  (peeled and cored)

For dressing:
2-3 tblsp. olive oil
½ tblsp. black-currant jelly
1½ tblsp. wine vinegar or
  dry white wine
pinch sugar

pepper and salt
a spoonful of yoghourt
  or sour cream improves
  the dressing

Soak salt herrings overnight in cold water to which a little milk has been added. Dry and fillet. Chop up herrings into very small pieces, also chop hard-boiled eggs, gherkin, potatoes, apples, beetroot and shred onion.

Mix well.

Make up dressing, blend and pour over salad. Leave in refrigerator overnight and serve chilled.

Rollmops-Savoury Raw Herrings

3 salt herrings	a little French mustard
2-3 pickled gherkin	peppercorns
1 small onion	wine vinegar
1 bay leaf	pinch sugar

Wash herrings and soak them for twenty-four hours in water to which a little milk has been added. Dry and fillet.

Put the fillets on a flat dish. Cover each with a layer of chopped gherkin, onion and a touch of mustard. Roll the fillets, tie with linen thread or hold together with small wooden skewer. Put fillets into an earthenware jar, cover with vinegar to which a few peppercorns, onion slices, a bay leaf and a pinch of sugar have been added. Cover closely and leave for two to three days in a cool place.

Serve chilled with brown bread or hot toast.

John Dory with Tartar Sauce

4 John Dory fillets
2 tblsp. flour

3 tblsp. vegetable oil
pepper and salt

Turn fish in flour to which pepper and salt have been added.
Fry in oil until brown and crisp on both sides.

For Sauce Tartare:

2 egg yolks
3 small finely
  chopped onions
1 tblsp. chopped
  pickled gherkins
1 tblsp. chopped capers

1 tblsp. chopped parsley
a little taragon
1 tsp. wine vinegar
½ tsp. French mustard
3 tbsp. olive oil
pepper and salt

Put egg yolks into bowl with a little salt and pepper, carefully
adding vinegar and olive oil, drop by drop, using a wooden
spoon, beating until sauce thickens. Carefully blend in rest of
ingredients. Pour over fried fish or serve in a separate dish.

Haddock with Mustard Butter

1 good-size haddock (on the bone)

For the Mustard Butter:

2 tblsp. butter
1 tblsp. French mustard

pinch sugar
pepper and salt

Cook haddock in court-bouillon until tender. Drain and keep hot.

Slightly heat butter over steam, add mustard and other ingredients and whip for three minutes. Pour over fish and serve very hot.

Parsley may be added, if desired.

Halibut Casserole

4 halibut steaks
1 green pepper
1 small onion
1 stick celery
1 small tin tomato purée
pinch sugar

a mixture of chopped
   marjoram and taragon
1 cup breadcrumbs
½ cup grated cheese
salt
2 tblsp. butter or
   vegetable oil

Gently fry sliced pepper, onion and celery in heated butter, add tomato purée, pinch of sugar, marjoram and taragon. Simmer for some ten minutes. Put halibut steaks into greased casserole and pour over mixture. Top with well blended breadcrumbs and grated cheese to which a little salt has been added. Bake in moderate oven for some thirty minutes.

Mackerel cooked with White Wine

2 good-size mackerel
2 small onions
1 cup cleaned and
   chopped mushrooms
1 glass white wine

2 tblsp. vegetable oil
1 bay leaf
chopped parsley
pepper and salt

Part cook mackerel in court-bouillon. Slightly fry chopped onions and mushrooms in vegetable oil, moisten with wine and add bay leaf, parsley and seasoning. Add fish, well drained, and continue cooking until done. Serve in its own liquid.

Fried Plaice

4 medium-size plaice
3 tblsp. flour

2 tblsp. butter or
   vegetable oil
pepper and salt

Clean fish and turn in flour to which pepper and salt have been added. Fry in heated butter until well done and brown on both sides.
Serve at once.

Raie au Beurre Noir
Skate with Caper Butter

1 lb. skate
3-4 tblsp. butter
½ glass white wine

capers
chopped parsley
pepper and salt

Simmer fish in court-bouillon for fifteen to twenty minutes.
Drain carefully and keep hot. Brown butter until almost black—
avoid burning—then take pan off flame and slowly add wine.
Season and add capers and parsley. Continue cooking for a
minute or two. Pour mixture over the fish and serve at once.

Sole in White Wine Sauce

6-8 fillets of sole
3 tomatoes
2 onions
1 cup mushrooms
2 cups white wine

2 tblsp. butter
1-1½ tblsp. flour
pinch sugar
parsley
pepper and salt

Clean and slice onions, tomatoes and mushrooms. Fry
slightly in heated butter. Slowly moisten with wine. Put in fish
fillets, season and simmer gently until fish is tender. Remove
fish, keep it hot, and thicken liquid with flour. Finish cooking,
and pour sauce over the fish. Serve very hot, sprinkled with
parsley.

Trout with Herb Sauce

4 trout
2 tblsp. butter
1 small onion
some fennel

parsley
squeeze lemon juice
2 slices white bread
pepper and salt

Clean trout and simmer in a court-bouillon for some fifteen minutes.

For the sauce:
Brown chopped onion in heated butter, adding fennel and parsley. Soak bread in a little of the court-bouillon, squeeze and add, together with half a cup of the court-bouillon to the herb mixture. Season, adding a squeeze of lemon juice. Blend well and simmer for another few minutes. Drain trout, cover with sauce and serve at once.

Whiting in Tomato Sauce

4 small whole whitings
1 small tin of tomato purée
2 tblsp. butter
pinch sugar

1 small onion
chopped parsley
pepper and salt

Prepare the whitings and place them in a buttered casserole. Season and cover with chopped onion and parsley. Add tomato purée and a pinch of sugar. Dot with butter and cook in a moderate oven for thirty minutes.

Continental Fish Balls

1-1½ lb. filleted
   white fish
1 large onion
2 eggs

1 cup breadcrumbs
a little parsley
pepper and salt

Steam fish in a court-bouillon till tender but not too soft. Let cool and flake. Chop onion very finely and add fish, breadcrumbs and seasoning. Bind with eggs, and shape mixture into small balls. Boil steadily, but not too quickly, for five to ten minutes in slightly salted water.

Serve hot with spinach or cold with a mixed salad and sauce tartare.

Ragout of Fish

4 fillets of cod
1 tblsp. butter
2 tblsp. flour

squeeze lemon juice
paprika
salt

Make sauce of butter, flour and water. Season with lemon juice, paprika and salt. Steam fish, fork it into small pieces and finish cooking in the sauce.

Serve hot with mashed potatoes and a side salad.

It may also be chilled and served cold on a bed of lettuce leaves.

Fish Casserole

4 fillets of any white fish
1 tblsp. flour
2 tblsp. butter
juice of half a lemon
1 small tin of tomato purée or a glass of
  white wine

1 small onion
chopped parsley
pepper and salt

Sprinkle fish with salt and pepper, chopped onion and parsley. Moisten with lemon juice. Roll up and place fillets closely together in a casserole. Dot with little lumps of butter. Cook in a medium oven for about half an hour. Make a sauce of flour, butter, purée or wine, using a little of the liquid which has collected in the casserole. Remove lid from casserole, cover fish with the sauce and continue cooking for some ten minutes until sauce browns on top.

Serve with boiled potatoes and a side salad.

Steamed Fish on Vegetables

4 fillets of haddock
1 lb. carrots
½ medium-size cabbage

1 tablsp. butter
pepper and salt

Clean and cook vegetables—in as little water as possible—until half tender. Then place fish on top with little lumps of butter. Season and finish cooking on low flame.

Serve with boiled potatoes.

The dish may be served with white sauce made from the vegetable and fish juice with the addition of a little white wine.

Cauliflower and Fish Pudding

1 medium-size cauliflower
4 fish fillets
  (any white fish)
1 cup milk
2 tblsp. butter
1 egg

½ cup grated cheese
½ cup breadcrumbs
squeeze lemon juice
pinch sugar
pepper and salt

Cook cauliflower in boiling water to which a pinch of sugar has been added. Remove from water before quite soft and drain. Moisten fish fillets with lemon juice, place in greased oven dish and cover with broken-up cauliflower. Switch up egg with milk, pepper and salt, and pour over dish. Cover with mixture of crumbs and grated cheese, dotting with lumps of butter. Bake in moderate oven for some twenty-five minutes.

Leeks with Cheese and Paprika

5-6 good-size leeks (the white part only, while the green can be used for soup)

2 tblsp. flour

1 tblsp. butter

1 tblsp. grated cheese

1 tsp. paprika

salt

   Clean and cut up leeks. Blanch in boiling water. Drain when tender but not too soft. Make white sauce of flour, butter and a little of the water the leeks have been cooked in, slowly adding grated cheese. Simmer leeks in the sauce for about another five minutes, add paprika and serve very hot.

Anchovy Eggs

4 eggs
1 small tin
   filleted anchovies

2 tblsp. butter
a few capers
pepper and salt

Hard-boil eggs. Cut into halves and remove yolks. Mix yolks with creamed butter and finely chopped anchovies. Season and refill eggs with the mixture. Garnish with capers and serve on lettuce leaves with hot buttered toast or thin brown bread.

Savoury Eggs

3 eggs
2 slices ham or
   left-over roast

French mustard
pepper and salt

Hard-boil eggs, cut into halves and remove yolks. Mince ham or roast, mix with mashed yolks, season, and heap mixture into halved eggs. Serve on a bed of lettuce or with cold meats and a mixed salad.

The dish may be varied by using sardines, steamed fish or cooked chopped-up mushrooms in place of meat.

Scrambled Eggs with Bückling (Smoked herring)

4 eggs
1 Bückling (or any
   type of bloater)
2 tblsp. butter

a little milk
pepper and salt
parsley

Skin and bone bückling and break it into small pieces. Fry these in butter, turning frequently. Beat the eggs with a little milk, pepper and salt. Pour them over the fish and continue cooking on a very low flame. When set, serve at once with hot toast.

Scrambled Eggs with Tomato and Chives

4 eggs
2 tomatoes
1 tblsp. butter

chopped chives
pepper and salt

Heat butter in frying pan. When brown, pour in eggs, switched-up with skinned and sliced tomatoes and chives. Scramble when mixture begins to set. Serve very hot with sauté potatoes or on toast.

Fairy Toadstools
Tomatoes and Eggs

4 eggs
2 tomatoes
a little mayonnaise
lettuce
1 cup cooked shrimps, tinned sardines or thin slices of smoked salmon)
pepper and salt

Hard-boil eggs, then remove a small slice from the bottom of each egg so that it will stand upright. Cut tomatoes into halves and scoop out centres. Put one half over each egg (this gives the eggs the appearance of toadstools). Decorate the tops with tiny spots of mayonnaise. Mix shrimps or sardines with a little mayonnaise, pepper and salt, and arrange the mixture round the eggs on leaves of lettuce. If smoked salmon is used, this should be arranged in thin slices round the eggs, dotted with mayonnaise.

Hunter's Breakfast

3-4 eggs
3-4 cooked potatoes
2 onions
pepper and salt

any left-overs (meats,
    fish, mushrooms)
vegetable oil

Slice onions and potatoes and fry in heated oil until golden brown. Add bits and pieces, beat up eggs and pour over the mixture. Leave on fire until eggs have set.

Serve very hot.

This may be accompanied by hot vegetables or a mixed salad.

Gnocchi-Semolina Dumplings

1 cup semolina	grated cheese (preferably
2 cups milk	Parmesan or Gruyère)
2 eggs	salt
2 tblsp. butter	

Bring milk to the boil, and cook semolina until thick and smooth. Add half the butter and salt. Remove from fire and add eggs. Mix well. When quite cool, shape into small balls, flatten, turn in grated cheese and fry in remaining butter till golden brown on both sides.

Serve hot.

Tomato sauce may be served with this, and thyme and nutmeg added to the mixture before frying.

Czech Cheese Paste

2 tblsp. grated cheese	1 small onion
2 tblsp. butter	paprika
1 tblsp. milk	

Cream butter, slowly adding grated cheese, finely chopped onion and paprika. Blend well until very creamy. Let cool before spreading on hot toast, rolls or sandwich fingers.

This is also a good stuffing for tomatoes or potatoes.

Tomato Savoury

6 tomatoes
1 onion
1 tblsp. butter
a little milk
breadcrumbs

1 cup grated cheese
mixed herbs
pinch sugar
pepper and salt

Drop tomatoes into boiling water for a minute or two and remove skin. Cut them into thick slices. Brown chopped onion in butter, add tomatoes and cook, stirring all the time. Carefully add breadcrumbs, milk and seasoning. Put into well-greased casserole, cover with grated cheese and bake in a moderate oven for some forty minutes.

Liver Paté

½ lb. liver (calf's, lamb's, possibly mixed with chicken liver)
1 tblsp. butter
1 clove garlic
2 whole cloves
pinch sugar
pepper and salt
a little marjoram, thyme and sage

Cook liver with chopped garlic and a pinch of sugar—until soft—in enough water to cover. When tender, cool, dry and mince finely. Mix with melted butter, season with the rest of ingredients, and stir for five minutes over steam. Put into earthenware dish, press well down, pour a little melted butter over it, and keep in a cool place. Serve with crisp toast or thin slices of brown bread.

Especially good with Continental rye bread. Garnish, if desired, with thin slices of pickled gherkin.

Pork Jelly

1-1½ lb. pork (not too fat, with a few bones)	1 onion
	mixed herbs
	2 bay leaves
2-3 carrots	a little white wine
1 potato	pepper and salt

Put meat into saucepan with the bones, adding cut-up vegetables and seasoning. Cover with equal parts of wine and water. Bring quickly to the boil, then simmer gently till meat is tender. Skim, cut meat into slices and put into a flat dish with vegetables arranged around the meat. Pour over strained liquid, and when cool place in refrigerator. Let the jelly set overnight, and then cut into small squares with a sharp knife.

Serve with salad or by itself as an hors d'oeuvre.

Béchamel Potatoes

6 good-size potatoes
a few rashers bacon
1 cup milk
1 small onion

2 tblsp. flour
1 tblsp. butter
pinch grated nutmeg
pepper and salt

Boil potatoes in their jackets. Peel and cut into thick slices. Crisp-up cubed bacon in frying pan, add butter and finely chopped onion. Cook till golden brown. Lower flame, add flour and milk carefully and finish cooking. Season with nutmeg, pepper and salt, then putting potato slices—which should be kept hot on the side of the stove—and simmer for a little. Serve very hot.

Gratin Dauphinois Cheese Potatoes

6 good-size potatoes
1 cup grated cheese
   (preferably Gruyère)
1 egg
2 cups milk

½ clove garlic
butter
pinch grated nutmeg
pepper and salt
a little thyme

Peel and slice thinly raw potatoes. Put them into buttered casserole, Chop garlic and distribute it over potatoes, also thyme, nutmeg, pepper and salt. Blend egg, milk and half the cheese, and mix with potatoes. Sprinkle top with the rest of the cheese, adding dots of butter. Cook in moderate oven for some forty minutes till potato slices are well done and the top brown and crisp. Serve very hot.

Risi e Bisi -Rice and Peas

2 cups rice
2 cups small peas
3 tblsp. butter

grated cheese
pepper and salt

Cook rice and peas separately. Drain peas, add to cooked rice together with butter and seasoning. Simmer gently for a few minutes. Sprinkle with grated cheese and serve at once.

Chilled, this dish may form the basis for a savoury rice salad.

Shrimps with Beetroot and hard-boiled Eggs

1 cup cooked shrimps
2 hard-boiled eggs
2 medium-size
   cooked beetroot

1 small onion
mayonnaise
pepper and salt

Mix shrimps with grated onion, seasoning and mayonnaise. Heap mixture on rounds of buttered toast and surround with slices of beetroot and hard-boiled egg.

Cold Meats in Mayonnaise

Slices of cold roast, salame, cold ham—in fact, any meat left-overs
2 peeled and sliced tomatoes
2 cooked sliced beetroot
any left-over cooked peas, carrots, asparagus or mushrooms
1 tsp. chopped parsley
1 tsp. chopped chives
½ tsp. chopped tarragon
mayonnaise

Chop up meats and mix with vegetables. Season and chill. Keep mayonnaise ready and mix well with rest of ingredients, just before serving. Sprinkle with herbs.

Vegetable Aspic

1 cup peas
6 small carrots
a few asparagus
   tips or mushrooms

1½-2 tblsp. gelatine
squeeze lemon juice
pinch sugar
pepper and salt

Cook vegetables in the usual way, adding a squeeze of lemon juice, a little sugar, pepper and salt to water. Drain vegetables when tender, using the water in which they have been cooked to make a jelly. Arrange the vegetables in a flat dish, pour over the jelly and leave to set.
Serve chilled as accompaniment to cold meats.

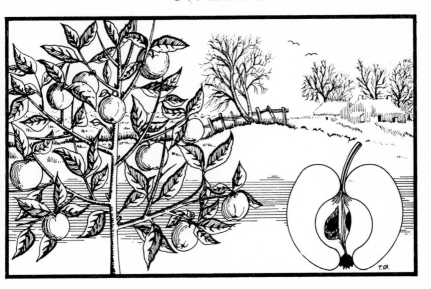

Apple Snow

4 good-size apples
2 tblsp. sugar
grated lemon peel

whites of two eggs
2 tblsp. cream

    Stew apples slowly with sugar. Rub through sieve. Add lemon peel and let cool. Then blend with whites of eggs, stiffly beaten, and gently stir in cream.
    Serve chilled.

Snowy Milk

| 4 cups milk | 2 tblsp. sugar |
| 2 eggs | vanilla |

Separate the egg yolks from the whites. Put yolks, sugar, vanilla and milk into deep bowl. Mix well and transfer to large saucepan. Bring to boiling point—do not let boil—. Remove from heat and drop stiffly beaten egg whites from spoon on top of liquid. Return to very low flame until whites have set. Allow to cool, and serve well chilled in tall glasses with spoons. Sprinkle with ground cinnamon if desired.

Black Currant and Raspberry Mousse

⸍. black currants	2 whites of egg
'b. raspberries	1 cup cream
⸍ʋ sugar	

⸍ ⸍ʋk black currants in little water until soft. Let cool. Then mix with raw washed rasperries, sugar and mix with two well-whisked whites of egg. Fold in cream, put into refrigerator and serve chilled.

This can also be successfully frozen.

Wine Jelly

¾ litre white wine
   or cider
3-4 tsp. gelatine

1 cup fresh cream
2 tblsp. sugar

Slightly heat sugared wine and melt gelatine in it. Chill and before mixture sets, whisk in cream. Serve well cooled.
The jelly may be decorated with sliced bananas.

Fruit and Cream Cheese

1 lb. cream cheese
1 cup milk
1 cup cream
sugar

squeeze lemon juice
1 lb. of any berry
   fruit available

Whisk cream cheese with milk, cream, a little sugar and lemon juice. Wash fruit carefully and sprinkle with sugar. with the rest of ingredients, place into refrigerator and serve well chilled.

Stuffed Melon

1 good-size melon
mixed fresh fruit (strawberries, raspberries, brambles or ripe
peaches, apricots and grapes)
juice of half a lemon
sugar
a small glass Kirsch or Grand Marnier

Cut off top of melon and scoop out flesh, removing the seeds.
Cube flesh and mix with fruit, sugar, lemon juice and spirits. Refill the melon with this fruit salad and place in refrigerator. Serve
well chilled.

Creamed Rice with Apricots

1 lb. rice
1 litre milk
1½ tblsp. sugar
1 tsp. butter

pinch salt
1 vanilla pod
1 cup stewed apricots

Wash rice, blanch in boiling water, drain, rinse in cold water
and drain again. Put rice into saucepan with a litre of boiled
milk, add pinch of salt, vanilla pod and sugar. Simmer gently
for half an hour. Remove from fire and add butter and apricots.
Mix well, return to fire and cook for another five minutes.
Remove vanilla pod.

Serve chilled, decorated with whipped cream.

Swiss Muesli

2-6 tblsp. crushed oats
2 apples
1 tblsp. honey

4 tblsp. rich milk
squeeze lemon juice
chopped nuts

Soak oats overnight. Next morning mix with milk, honey, unpeeled grated apples, nuts and a squeeze of lemon juice.
Serve at once.
This is an excellent breakfast dish but it may also be served as a sweet.

Buttermilk Sweet

1 litre buttermilk
½ cup sugar

3-4 tblsp. gelatine
grated lemon peel

Sugar the buttermilk and slowly add melted gelatine. Stir well and flavour with lemon peel.
Leave to set and serve chilled.
Decorate with whipped cream and grated nuts.

Banana Crème

2 eggs
2 bananas
1 tsp. brown sugar

1 tsp. rum
a little gelatine

Mix well yolks of eggs, peeled and mashed bananas. Flavour with sugar and rum. Stir into the mixture a little gelatine melted in half a cup of warm water. Switch up whites of eggs and fold carefully into the crème.

Chill and serve in individual glasses, decorated with whipped cream.

Coffee Crème

2 cups strong black coffee	2 tblsp. vanilla
1 cup milk	flavoured-sugar
2 eggs	1-1½ tsp. gelatine

Bring to the boil milk to which the strained sugared coffee has been added. Let cool, and when lukewarm add well-beaten egg yolks. Continue cooking gently, stirring with wooden spoon. Remove from fire, and add melted gelatine and fold in beaten egg whites. Chill and serve decorated with grated chocolate.

Whipped cream and chopped almonds may serve as an alternative decoration.

Sweet of Stewed Prunes

½ lb. dried prunes (stewed)
½ cup double cream
3-4 rusks

Rub stewed prunes through sieve, crush rusks and moisten with juice of prunes. Put purée of prunes and moistened rusks in alternate layers into individual glasses. Cover with whipped cream.

Arme Ritter Toast

4 thick slices French bread
2 eggs
1 cup milk
1 tblsp. brown sugar

2 tblsp. butter
a little castor sugar
ground cinnamon

Whip up sweetened milk and eggs. Turn slices in the mixture, taking care that bread does not get too soft. Fry slices in butter till golden brown on both sides. Sprinkle with castor sugar and cinnamon.
Serve with stewed fruit.
A little brandy added to the sweetened milk improves the dish.

Doughnuts in Wine Sauce

2 eggs
2 tblsp. sugar
1 tblsp. butter
2 cups plain flour

1 cup warm milk
1 tsp. yeast
pinch salt
vegetable oil

Mix well flour, salt, butter and sugar. Dissolve yeast in warm milk and add to the dough. Cover and let rise for half an hour. Add beaten eggs and let rise again for about an hour in a warm place.

Drop spoonfuls of the batter into deep (boiling) oil and fry quickly till golden brown. Lift out on to a hot dish and serve covered with wine sauce.

Ingredients for Sauce:

½ bottle white wine or cider
2 eggs

1 tblsp. sugar
squeeze lemon juice

Mix all ingredients in a basin and stand in a saucepan of boiling water.

Beat till frothy.

The doughnuts can also be served cold, without sauce, sprinkled with castor sugar.

Kaiserschmarrn
Austrian Broken Pancake

3 eggs
2 tblsp. flour (if plain flour, add a tsp. baking powder)
½ cup milk
1 handful sultanas or raisins
pinch salt
1 tblsp. sugar
butter

Blend flour and milk into a batter, add yolks of eggs, salt, a little melted butter and finally the whites of eggs beaten stiff.

Heat butter well in frying pan, pour in batter sprinkle with raisins and cook till golden brown on both sides. Before serving, fork pancake into irregular pieces and dust over with castor sugar.

Thin slices of raw apples, sprinkled with cinnamon may be used instead of sultanas or raisins.

'Veiled Lady' Fruit Pie

3-4 slices golden
   brown toast
2 tblsp. butter
2 tblsp. sugar

2 cups milk
1 egg
1 cup stewed fruit
a little ground cinnamon

Grease oven dish, butter toast and place in bottom of dish, sprinkling with cinnamon. Mix yolk of egg with milk and half the sugar. Pour this over toast. Cook over steam for about twenty-five minutes. Whisk white of egg with rest of sugar, mix with stewed fruit and put on top of cooked ingredients. Finish cooking in moderate oven for about half an hour.

Serve hot.

Fruit Pie with Porridge Oats

3-4 cups stewed fruit (made from fresh or dried fruit)
3 cups rolled porridge oats
1 cup milk
1 egg
2 tblsp. sugar
1 tblsp. grated almonds

Put alternate layers of fruit and oats into an oven dish, making the top layer oats. Mix egg, milk, sugar and almonds, and pour over the layers. Bake in a moderate oven for about half an hour. Serve hot.

Slovak Jam Fritters

2-3 eggs
1 cup flour
½ cup milk
1 tsp. butter
1 tsp. brandy

jam
castor sugar
poppy seeds
pinch salt

Mix well eggs, flour, butter, milk and brandy with a pinch of salt. Add a little water to make a fairly thick dough. Knead and roll out on pastry board. Cut into squares, spread one half with jam and fold over the other half. Sprinkle with poppy seed and quick-fry in hot oil.
Serve sprinkled with sugar.

Apfelstrudel

3 cups flour
½ cup sugar
2 eggs
2 tblsp. butter
a little lukewarm water
pinch salt

5 cups sliced apples
½ cup raisins
1 cup fried breadcrumbs
½ tsp. ground cinnamon
squeeze lemon juice

Mix flour, salt and butter, adding eggs and enough water to make an elastic dough. Knead well for fifteen minutes until dough shows bubbles on top, and comes easily off the hands. Put mixture into a basin, cover with cloth and keep in a warm place for about forty-five minutes. Put a large clean cloth on kitchen table, sprinkle with flour and roll out dough on it. Lift up dough and stretch carefully till very thin. Trim off any thick edges, brush dough with melted butter and spread with apples, raisins and breadcrumbs, flavoured with lemon juice, sugar and cinnamon. Lift up cloth and roll up strudel. Bend into horseshoe shape and place on a greased baking-tray. Brush over with melted butter and bake in moderate oven till golden brown. Sprinkle with castor sugar and serve hot.

CAKES AND CUP DRINKS

Dutch Honey Cake

2 cups flour	1 tblsp. butter
1 cup honey	2 tsp. baking powder
½ cup sugar	2 tsp. mixed spice
½ cup milk	½ cup mixed peel

Slowly melt honey and butter in milk, carefully sifting in flour, baking powder and other ingredients. Put into well greased tin and bake in a moderate oven for about forty minutes. Sprinkle thickly with sugar just before removing from oven.

Fruit Cake

1½ cups flour
1 tblsp. butter
2 eggs
1 cup milk
½ tblsp. sugar

a little cinnamon
½ tsp. yeast
1 lb. apples, damsons
   or plums
castor sugar

Mix yeast with a little lukewarm milk and a pinch of sugar. Put flour into a deep bowl, making a well in the centre. Put in the dissolved yeast and mix slowly and carefully with a little of the surrounding flour. Cover bowl and let centre dough rise in a warm place until doubled. Then add other ingredients—the butter creamed—and let the mixture rise again. When dough has doubled, roll it out and put it on a flat greased baking-tray. Cover with peeled and sliced raw apples or stoned damsons or plums, cut into halves. Mix sugar with ground cinnamon and sprinkle over the fruit, then dot with small lumps of butter.

Bake in moderate oven for about thirty minutes. If fruit is not very sweet, let cool, and sprinkle with castor sugar before serving.

Fruit Shortcake

2 cups flour
2 tsp. baking powder
2 tblsp. butter
1 tblsp. sugar

1 egg
pinch salt
1 tblsp. water

For filling:
1 lb. strawberries
a little gelatine

Put flour with baking powder into deep bowl, make well in centre and put in whole egg, adding butter, salt, sugar and water. Knead thoroughly, roll out. Bake in greased round tin, for about thirty minutes in moderate oven.

When cool, fill with strawberries: one part crushed and sugared, one part slightly stewed, the liquid thickened with gelatine.

Decorate with whipped cream, if desired.

Gugelhupf-Viennese Yeast Cake

3 cups flour
2 tblsp. butter
2 eggs
1 tblsp. oil

2 tblsp. sugar
2 tblsp. raisins
abbout 1 tsp. yeast
castor sugar

Mix yeast with a little lukewarm milk and pinch of sugar. Put flour into deep bowl, making a well in the centre. Put the dissolved yeast into this and mix slowly and carefully with a little of the surrounding flour. Cover bowl with clean cloth and leave in a warm place until centre dough has doubled. Then add the remaining milk, sugar, eggs and melted butter. Stir well, adding the raisins last. Finish kneading on a floured baking-board. Put into a well-greased baking-tin, leaving enough space for the dough to double. Cover and leave to rise again in a warm place for an hour.

Bake in moderate oven for some fifty to sixty minutes.
Serve sprinkled with castor sugar.

Kranzkuchen-Garland Cake

1½ cups flour
1½ tblsp. butter
1½ tblsp. sugar
1 cup milk

2 eggs
1-1½ tsp. yeast
2 cups raisins, grated
    nuts and chopped peel

Mix yeast with a little lukewarm milk and a pinch of sugar. Put flour into deep bowl, making a well in the centre. Put the dissolved yeast into this and mix slowly and carefully with a little of the surrounding flour. Cover bowl and let the centre dough rise until doubled. Then add other ingredients—the butter creamed—. Knead thoroughly and roll out mixture on a floured cloth on the kitchen table.

Brush over with melted butter and sprinkle with raisins, nuts and peel. Roll up the dough into a long thin sausage. Cut into halves and plait the two rolls together. Put on a greased baking-tray, cover and let rise again.

Bake in a moderate oven until golden brown.

Sprinkle with castor sugar or cover with white icing when it comes out of oven.

Streuselkuchen
German Yeast Cake

1½ cups flour
2 tblsp. butter
2 eggs
1½ cups milk

2 tblsp. sugar
pinch salt
½ tsp. yeast

For the top:
1 tblsp. butter
2 tblsp. flour

1 tblsp. sugar
a little cinnamon

Mix yeast with a little lukewarm milk and a pinch of sugar. Put flour into deep bowl, making a well in the centre. Put the dissolved yeast into this and mix slowly and carefully with a little of the surrounding flour. Cover bowl with clean cloth and let centre dough rise in a warm place until doubled. Add other ingredients and allow to rise again. When dough has doubled in bulk, roll out and put on a flat greased baking-tray. Then melt butter for top in saucepan, add flour sugar and cinnamon. Shake over heat until little balls form. Put these on the rolled-out dough and bake in moderate oven for about thirty to forty minutes.

Iced Coffee

½ litre strong coffee
½ litre milk
3 tblsp. brown sugar

a little vanilla
whipped cream

Bring milk to the boil, adding a little vanilla. Let cool, sweeten and mix with coffee. Stir well before putting into refrigerator for a couple of hours. Serve well chilled—but not stiff—in individual glasses, topped with whipped cream.

A teaspon of whisky, brandy or kirsch may be added to each glass.

Fruit Milk

1 litre milk
½ litre fresh fruit juice (from berries put through liquidiser)
sugar

Sweeten fruit juice and blend well with milk, taking care that milk does not curdle. This is best done in electric blender. Serve chilled. This may be topped with whipped cream to which a little sugar and vanilla have been added.

Fruit Cup

1 bottle medium-dry white wine
½ bottle soda water (champagne is, of course, much better!)
1 small glass brandy or white rum
2 tblsp. sugar
1 lb. strawberries or 3-4 peaches, peeled, stoned and sliced thinly

Put the fruit, carefully washed and dried, into a deep bowl, sprinkle with sugar, pour over brandy and leave in refrigerator for a few hours. Then add wine and return to refrigerator for about one hour. Take out and add soda water just before serving. Put some fruit into each individual glass and provide small spoons. Sweet oranges and fresh pineapple are equally good for fruit cups.

Lemon Cup

1 bottle white wine
½ bottle soda water
2 tblsp. sugar

juice of one lemon
lemon peel

Melt sugar and mix with lemon juice, add to wine and pour the mixture into a lemonade jug. Peel a lemon very thinly, taking care to keep the peel all in one. Plunge the peel into the jug, and place into refrigerator for about half an hour. Then add soda water and serve at once.

May Cup

1 bottle white wine
½ bottle soda water
sugar (don't oversweeten)
1 small glass brandy
1 small bunch freshly picked woodruff
(in season in May, hence the name). Must be picked before flowering

Wash and dry woodruff. Sugar slightly and place into deep bowl. Pour over brandy and put into refrigerator for three to four hours. Add wine and return to refrigerator for about an hour. Take out, remove woodruff, add soda water and serve at once. Again, champagne or Asti Spumante greatly improves the cup.

Herbs and their Uses

Aniseed:	sweets and cakes
Balm—Lemon Balm	salads, omelettes, sauces to go with fish. Also good in fruit cups.
Basil:	shredded in tomato salad; flavours soups, roasts and sauces.
Bay leaf	flavouring many dishes, particularly soups, fish, stews and sauces.
Bergamot:	shredded in salads.
Borage:	chopped leaves in cucumber salad. Flowers in cup drinks.
Caraway:	seeds in stews, cream cheese, cakes and bread.
Chervil:	chopped leaves in omelettes, stews, soups and sauces.

Chives:	wherever a mild onion flavour is required. Freshly chopped on clear soups.
Coriander:	seeds in chutneys and curries.
Costmary:	chopped leaves in soups and salads.
Dill:	leaves and seeds for fish dishes and sauces.
Fennel:	fish, pork and veal (leaves) cucumber salad and pickled gherkin (seeds)
Garlic:	cloves sparingly used in any savoury dish
Hyssop:	stews and salads
Lovage:	salads and soups
Marjoram:	soups, stews, omelettes, meats.
Mint (all varieties):	young summer vegetables, sauces, lamb, summer drinks.
Parsley:	meats, fish, omelettes, soups, sauces and as garnish.
Rosemary:	meats, poultry, fish and in stuffings.
Sage:	meats, poultry and in stuffings.
Summer Savoury:	soups, meats, salads and omelettes.
Sorrel, French:	fresh leaves in salads and omelettes. Cooked as a purée, with pork and veal.

Tarragon:	soups, salads, herb mayonnaise and added to wine vinegar.
Thyme:	soups, meats vegetables, poultry and stews.

Common Spices:

Cinammon:	cakes, sweets.
Cloves:	stewing apples, pears and plums. Baking ham and with stews.
Ginger:	cakes, spinach, rubbing meat for roasting.
Juniper berries:	sauerkraut and for beetroot pickling.
Nutmeg:	spinach, white sauces, milk puddings.
Paprika:	wherever a strong pepper flavour is required.

INDEX